THE LAST SALVATION TABLE

How to live the Divine Mercy today

Peter CS

© Peter CS

1st edition: March 2020

Introduction 9

First part: Mercy, Eucharist, Mercy... 11
   1. Jesus I trust in You, and the image of the Divine Mercy 11
   2. The origin and impulse of the Chaplet of the Divine Mercy 15
   3. How to say the Chaplet of the Divine Mercy? 17
   4. Devotions should serve us to approach God where He can be found: in the sacraments and especially the Mass 21
   5. Jesus risen, that is present with us in the Mass and in the Tabernacle, calls us to love 23
   6. Peace that Jesus brings and that transforms into joy 25
   7. What to do when we lose peace 27
   8. Trust in the sacrament of forgiveness 29
   9. Live the prayer in works of mercy 31
   10. Unafraid commitment 33

Second part: Living mercy 35
   11. The spirit of service that Jesus teaches us 35
   12. What do You want from me, my Lord? 37
   13. Avoid gossiping 39
   14. Jesus' patience 41
   15. Dedicate time to friendship with Jesus 43
   16. Jesus' message: Do not be afraid 45
   17. Go to Mass with devotion 47
   18. That technology doesn't make us lose love 51
   19. Do we love Jesus, or not? 53
   20. Ways to pray 55

Part Three: Understanding Mercy — 57

21. The tempter wants us to move away from Jesus as their first objective — 57
22. Faith, a gift that sometimes is not accepted — 59
23. People get salvation and forgiveness for their sins from God's deep love — 61
24. Understand that after the cross comes the resurrection and the greatest life — 65
25. How to beat temptation — 67
26. The endless task of praying for others — 71
27. The temptations have one purpose: to separate us from the love of God — 75
28. Pray for peace and love in the family — 77
29. Why pray for vocations — 79
30. To do good and live a saintly life affects those near us and the whole world — 81

Fourth part: Be a part of mercy — 85

31. To each setback, a greater door to trust in Jesus — 85
32. Live with the essential and bring it to fullness — 87
33. Humility is necessary when we do good — 91
34. John Baptist shows us Jesus and how to make him enter our lives — 93
35. All saints agree with the devotion to the Mass — 95
36. Effort to enter through the narrow door — 97
37. You can tell what they are by what they do — 101
38. The priority of the daily Mass, direct meeting with Jesus — 105
39. Confidence, the medicine of the soul — 107

Part five: Advancing in mercy — 109

40. You always move forward, although it may not seem obvious, from humility and sincere search for God and justice	109
41. Faith just as a mustard seed and its cultivation	113
42. Jesus' response to temptations	115
43. Offerings of suffering for those in need	119
44. Aridity for our sake	121
45. The communion of the saints and their help	123
46. Mary, full of grace	125
47. Invoking the Holy Spirit	127
48. Prayer renews us internally	131
49. What did Jesus do at moments of maximum pressure?	133
50. Mary, the perfect model to walk towards holiness	135

Part six: Examples of mercy — **137**

51. Saint John Bosco, holiness is joy	137
52. Saint Josemaría Escrivá, sanctity in the state of life, in our vocation, in our ordinary daily life	139
53. Saint Thérèse de Lisieux, the holiness that loves and offers itself to others	141
54. Saint Anthony Mary Claret and Saint Paul, the holiness of bringing the Gospel to the world	143
55. Saint John of God and Mother Teresa, the holiness of loving the forgotten	145
56. Saint Faustina Kowalska and Saint John Paul II, the holiness of bringing the mercy of God to the world	147
57. Saint Pius X, the sanctity of promoting the Eucharist	149
58. Saint Joseph, holiness in fidelity	151
59 Saint Augustine, the sanctity of rectification	153

60. Saint Joaquina Vedruna de Mas, the sanctity of educating, caring and loving others   157

Final words (the Epistle of Paul to the Colossians 3, 12-17)   159

Final prayer   161

Annex: Look at Jesus face to face   **163**

Introduction

Ever since I met the Chaplet of the Divine Mercy I said this prayer very frequently. She has allowed me to enter stronger into the Mass and to better understand the eternal present of God and the importance of the Eucharist, the source of all holiness.

This book is inspired by the experience of mercy and the urgency of living and sharing the Good News of the Gospel.

God asks us to share the message of love each according to their state and their charisma.

Thank you Lord. Thank you dear reader.

First part: Mercy, Eucharist, Mercy...

1. Jesus I trust in You, and the image of the Divine Mercy

A Polish priest told me that when Jesus asked Santa Faustina to paint a picture with his image, he did not ask to write: "Jesus, I love you" or "Jesus, protect me" or even "Jesus, have mercy. " He asked to write: "Jesus, I trust in You". Surely because Jesus detected a mistrust towards Him in many Christian layers of society and sometimes in ourselves.

Jesus promised to accompany humanity, He gave his life dying for us and revived. He's still alive and He becomes present in the Eucharist day after day. And in spite of these facts, which have many testimonies, many remain indifferent to the message and many who believe continue to be distrustful of Jesus and Divine Mercy and are not faithful enough to the commandments. Many also see how their faith is cooled in the midst of a liquid society. Maybe we have also found ourselves in this situation.

Jesus, therefore, like any friend who loves us, asks us for trust and always has the door open. He asks us to tell Him that we trust Him with a sincere and determined heart. And, we can do it, because it has never failed. We can do it with the brief prayer "Jesus, I trust in You". For this reason, from the image of Jesus of the Divine Mercy appears a red ray, symbol of the blood given to mankind for the forgiveness of sins, and a pale ray that means the water of Baptism, of renewal, the rescue from death towards life.

In His appearances to St. Faustina, Jesus trusts, as He has always done, in a humanity that sometimes does not trust. For that, He forgives seventy times seven those who repent and ask for forgiveness. Jesus does not get tired of forgiving.

Yes, Jesus wants to accompany us in our miseries and weaknesses so that, with your help, we can change and become those who are strong of faith and attentive in charity. Jesus is still prepared, waiting for the prodigal children, who are often ourselves.

Therefore, knowing Jesus our weakness, it is present in each Mass. That is why he invites us to go to Mass with as much as we can, because it is the greatest prayer, the sacrament in which Jesus, risen Jesus, is made present day after day.

If we can go to Mass every day, we will not go there only on Sundays. Today it's difficult for a Christian to live his faith from Sunday to Sunday. Jesus, however, invites us every day. It is the greatest prayer, the most important, the holy Mass. It is the encounter with Him, the great Friend, rescuer and our redeemer. And we also have Mary, the Mother of God, the perfect model of how we should behave and how we have to live our trust in Jesus.

Jesus, I trust in You.

2. The origin and impulse of the Chaplet of the Divine Mercy

Long time ago, in many parishes of Barcelona I saw the Jesus of Divine Mercy. I had heard about Santa Faustina's, but until a priest did not show me the prayer of the Chaplet, I did not quite understand the depth of the message and how good it is for us to say the Chaplet every day, to remember and implore Divine Mercy.

The Chaplet is the prayer around the Divine Mercy dictated by Jesus to Santa Faustina during September 13 and 14, 1935 in Vilnius (Lithuania), in a convulsive time in Europe and the world. In many sectors, the trust in God, love made mercy for mankind had diminished, vanity was empowering many people and violence was growing.

In this context and as always happens in situations where it seems that everything is lost, Jesus acts from humility. Santa Faustina was a nun from Poland. A simple person. Jesus relied on her to expand the message of mercy.

And the one who strongly promoted devotion to Divine Mercy was precisely the Polish Pope John Paul II, from his long lasting papacy. First, in 1980 with the encyclical "Dives in Mercy" and then in 2000, on April 30, instituting the feast of Divine Mercy on the first Sunday after Easter, a special day so that it could also canonize Santa Faustina Kowalska. Finally, on a trip in 2002 to Poland, John Paul II consecrated the world to Divine Mercy. Curiously, Pope Francis canonized Saint John Paul II and John XXIII on Sunday of Mercy in 2014, on April 27.

The Chaplet is said in about 8 minutes and is a prayer marked by the request of the mercy of God. Around the world this devotion is growing rapidly. And it already begins to be known in many parishes. Because far from being an isolated devotion, it is a source of return towards the Lord and drives the sacraments to live more strongly, more intensely and more lovingly, especially the sacraments of Forgiveness and Holy Mass.

The devotion to the Divine Mercy is like the great river that ends at the sea of the generous love of God that always waits for us at the end of each one of our miseries.

Jesus, I trust in You.

3. How to say the Chaplet of the Divine Mercy?

The way of saying the Chaplet of the Divine Mercy:

1. Make the Sign of the Cross
In the name of the Father, and of the Son, and of the Holy Spirit. Amen.

2. Optional Opening Prayers
You expired, Jesus, but the source of life gushed forth for souls, and the ocean of mercy opened up for the whole world. O Fount of Life, unfathomable Divine Mercy, envelop the whole world and empty Yourself out upon us.

(Repeat three times)
O Blood and Water, which gushed forth from the Heart of Jesus as a fount of mercy for us, I trust in You!

3. Our Father
Our Father, Who art in heaven, hallowed be Thy name; Thy kingdom come; Thy will be done on earth as it is in heaven. Give us this day our daily bread; and forgive us our trespasses as we forgive those who trespass against us; and lead us not into temptation, but deliver us from evil, Amen.

4. Hail Mary
Hail Mary, full of grace. The Lord is with thee. Blessed art thou amongst women, and blessed is the fruit of thy womb, Jesus. Holy Mary, Mother of God, pray for us sinners, now and at the hour of our death, Amen.

5. The Apostles' Creed
I believe in God, the Father almighty, Creator of heaven and earth, and in Jesus Christ, His only Son, our Lord, who was conceived by the Holy Spirit, born of the Virgin Mary, suffered under Pontius Pilate, was crucified, died and was buried; He descended into hell; on the third day He rose again from the dead; He ascended into heaven, and is seated at the right hand of God the Father almighty; from there He will come to judge the living and the dead. I believe in the Holy Spirit, the holy catholic Church, the communion of saints, the forgiveness of sins, the resurrection of the body, and life everlasting. Amen.

6. The Eternal Father
Eternal Father, I offer you the Body and Blood, Soul and Divinity of Your Dearly Beloved Son, Our Lord, Jesus Christ, in atonement for our sins and those of the whole world.

7. On the 10 Small Beads of Each Decade
For the sake of His sorrowful Passion, have mercy on us and on the whole world.

8. Repeat for the remaining decades
Saying the "Eternal Father" (6) on the "Our Father" bead and then 10 "For the sake of His sorrowful Passion" (7) on the following "Hail Mary" beads.

9. Conclude with Holy God (Repeat three times)
Holy God, Holy Mighty One, Holy Immortal One, have mercy on us and on the whole world.

10. Optional Closing Prayer
Eternal God, in whom mercy is endless and the treasury of compassion — inexhaustible, look kindly upon us and increase Your mercy in us, that in difficult moments we might not despair nor become despondent, but with great confidence submit ourselves to Your holy will, which is Love and Mercy itself.

Trust brings us peace and strength to move on. Some are praying it every day as the first prayer of the day, others at 3 in the afternoon, others later before the Eucharist... In any case, it is a simple and powerful prayer. Full of love, of the love of Jesus who died and resurrected for us. And who lives already full of glory to the right side of the Father, but does not forget about us, His dear ones. Just so we can live forever and be happy.

Jesus, I trust in You.

4. Devotions should serve us to approach God where He can be found: in the sacraments and especially the Mass

A devotion can't nor shouldn't be an obsession, but an effective mean of welcoming the love of God and encouraging us to live the sacraments more intensely.

Devotion to Divine Mercy is a call to humility and conversion, to realise the need we have of God and live according to His advice and His example of life.

Through the sacrament of confession and Mass, God renews us internally, in such a way that our life can be salt for the earth and light for the world.

In addition, devotion to Divine Mercy must also be open to works of mercy. Because faith without works is an empty faith.

Therefore, the Chaplet is a first step, it is an approach to God, a way to trust Him so we can come closer with more strength, more love, more humility, to the sacraments.

Divine Mercy is the reflection of Jesus' sufferings on the cross offered for our sake. That's why Jesus tells us: do not be afraid, no matter how hard you suffer, no matter how destroyed you feel inside, no matter how ruined your life seems to be, God wants to give you forgiveness and heal your wounds, because He is not here to call the righteous but the sinners. And He has overpowered death.

Jesus, I trust in You.

5. Jesus risen, that is present with us in the Mass and in the Tabernacle, calls us to love

The day the priest spoke to me about the Divine Mercy, he explained to me the dangers of having an external faith, but forget the center of faith, the risen Jesus, who is constantly offered to us. And He wants to shed His mercy.

Having devotion to saints and marian advocations is very opportune, but without forgetting that everything must be for the love of God, the One who loves us.

"God is love" tells St. John's letter. And this love has been so great that Jesus, true God and true man, came to the world and suffered for us. Just so love could triumph over evil.

Now, if we only had devotion in Mary or in the saints, we would not be understanding what Mary and the saints just exemplify: offer yourself to God humbly. Therefore Maria said: "Do whatever Jesus tells you to do" (Jn 2: 5).

Jesus, I trust in You.

We must come to Jesus
for peace + mercy on our soul.
It heals our wounds as
it flow through us as
we extend it to others
(thru forgiveness)

Know who Christ is!
(My Savior who frees me)
Know who I am
(a servant of God. I
must come to Him + ask)

Don't focus on my will =
" my feelings "
my thoughts "or judgements
of how a person should act
Focus on Gods will = forgiveness
I am a servant He is God

6. Peace that Jesus brings and that transforms into joy

The world needs peace. And to get it, Jesus says to Santa Faustina that you must go with confidence to His Divine Mercy.

We all seek peace. Peace is fundamental in our lives and for the progress in all fields of love. Jesus risen, when He greets, He does it in this way: "Peace be upon you".

The element of peace, the result of trust in mercy, reminds us that we must be leaders of peace for people. Inner peace and outer peace. And we have to work for justice, for every day to be more righteous and joyful.

St. Paul will say in three letters that we need to live joyfully: Always live happy in the Lord! I repeat it, live happily (Fl 4.4).

Sometimes, achieving peace can lead to an inner struggle, but Mary teaches us the path of victory: maximum humility, maximum confidence, maximum obedience.

If we want to do things in our own way, we will probably lose peace. But if being humble, we adapt to what the experts in each field offer us or send us, surely we will move forward and progress in such a way that feel peace and bring peace to others will be very normal in our life.

Jesus, I trust in You.

7. What to do when we lose peace

Sometimes we lose peace. For this reason, risen Jesus instigates the sacrament of confession to recover it. And He creates it in the first appearance to the disciples:

Then He breathed on them and said: "Receive the Holy Spirit. If you forgive anyone's sins, they will be forgiven. But if you don't forgive their sins, they will not be forgiven." (Jn 20, 22-23)

Therefore, it is important to understand that Jesus gives importance to people despite their flaws, wants to make them participate in the work of reconciliation. And in this case, He leaves it in the hands of the disciples.

Therefore, when we are going to confess, we are faced with the clear will of Jesus, who gives the apostles this ability to, through Him, give their mercy through the forgiveness of sins. It is an extraordinary gift. God loves us and wants to cure our wounds. And like that, He wants that once we're cured we can be bearers of hope in a world that always needs it.

If we entrust ourselves to Mary, if we pray to her, she will help us to quickly approach confession with total confidence.

Jesus, I trust in You.

8. Trust in the sacrament of forgiveness

We can not be afraid of the sacrament of mercy. Confession should make us grateful and be well prepared to receive Jesus in the Eucharist. For God, nothing is impossible, and even our misery can be converted. As St Paul said: where sin abounded, grace surpassed (letter from Saint Paul to Romans 5:20).

The goal of the evil people is that we discourage ourselves, that we lose precisely the trust in Jesus and in the sacraments that He himself instituted. Therefore, when there is a crisis in the sacrament of confession, there is a crisis in all the sacraments, because it is our pride what makes us say: I confess myself directly to God. But it is Jesus who wishes that we continue to trust in Him and in His Church.

Jesus did not jealously keep the protagonism but sought the mediation of the disciples so they could also experience the joy of being able to administer reconciliation.

Jesus, I trust in You.

9. Live the prayer in works of mercy

For our faith to be alive, we must pray and we must live what we pray. Often, in the practical experience of faith, we do not know how to suffer as Jesus did. And when we are presented with a contrariety or a cross, if we have the opportunity to throw it away, we want to do it to avoid suffering.

Even powerful and popular prayers, such as the Chaplet of Divine Mercy or the Rosary, are despised because of being too repetitive, when, in fact, all that is good, it is necessary to be repeated.

Both the Chaplet and the Rosary are the effective and recommended means to deepen our faith, renew our love and grow in charity. A way of communicating with God.

All devotions must end in the great devotion of the Eucharist, the source of all holiness. And if we have to choose between devotion and participate in the Eucharist, we must prioritize the Mass. There, Jesus becomes present and we have the most complete, communitarian and integral prayer.

The devotions are very good, but the great devotion, the number one priority must be to be able to participate in

Holy Mass and practice it to the fullest. Our hearts need the living water, the water that puts off our deep thirst.

With the Holy Mass, our hearts converted or fortified in charity must be prepared to love more at home, at work, friends, enemies... and think the same way that Christ Jesus thought (St. Paul's letter to the Philippians 2, 5).

Jesus, I trust in You.

10. Unafraid commitment

Jesus has committed himself so much and loves us so much, that he wants us to commit ourselves to love. Therefore, prayer is a simple beginning, to continue walking and to not get tired of doing works of mercy. With humility and simplicity.

The works of mercy are fourteen: seven bodily and seven spiritual.

The corporals are:
- To feed the hungry.
- To give water to the thirsty.
- To clothe the naked.
- To visit the imprisoned and the sick.
- To shelter the homeless.
- To ransom those who are captive.
- To bury the dead.

The spiritual ones:
- To instruct the ignorant.
- To give good advice to those who need it.
- To correct those who are wrong.
- To console the sad and heartbroken.
- To forgive insults.

- To patiently suffer the weaknesses and discomforts of those who surround us.
- To pray for the living and the dead.

Jesus, I trust in You.

Second part: Living mercy

11. The spirit of service that Jesus teaches us

To be active in works of mercy is to transfer in facts what Jesus summarizes in two commandments: to love God over all things and to others as oneself.

The passage of the Gospel of Marc is quite explicit (Mc 12, 28-34):
28 One of the teachers of the Law of Moses came up while Jesus and the Sadducees were arguing. When he heard Jesus give a good answer, he asked him, "What is the most important commandment?"
29 Jesus answered, "The most important one says: 'People of Israel, you have only one Lord and God.
30 You must love him with all your heart, soul, mind, and strength.' 31 The second most important commandment says: 'Love others as much as you love yourself.' No other commandment is more important than these."
32 The man replied, "Teacher, you are certainly right to say there is only one God.
33 It is also true that we must love God with all our heart, mind, and strength, and that we must love others as

much as we love ourselves. These commandments are more important than all the sacrifices and offerings that we could possibly make."

34 When Jesus saw that the man had given a sensible answer, he told him, "You are not far from God's kingdom."

A splendid but often forgotten synthesis. In a world that sometimes encourages us to forget about others for more comfort, the works of mercy prompt us to be servants and suffer with the sufferers using the total love of God that spills complete love towards others.

Prayings, particularly those said in Holy Mass, do not stop stressing the purpose of conversion of our hard core, so that it transforms into a humble heart, simple and able to truly love.

Jesus reminds us (Mt 7, 13): 13 "Go in through the narrow gate. The gate to destruction is wide, and the road that leads there is easy to follow. A lot of people go through that gate."

Jesus, I trust in You.

12. What do You want from me, my Lord?

Many are disconcerted by silence. It is in silence, and because of the trust we put in Jesus, that we are inspired to act in a certain way or to do certain works.

And it is in silence how we can enter prayer. One of the most popular is the Rosary, because it reviews the most important moments of Jesus' life, accompanied by Mary, the Virgin Mary.

We can easily find Saint Rosary on the internet. It's a prayer that lasts about 25 minutes. Depending on the day, we review mysteries of joy (Monday and Saturday), pain (Tuesday and Friday), glory (Wednesday and Sunday) and light (Thursday).

It is a magnificent review of Jesus' life and a simple teaching to understand all the mysteries of our faith.

In prayer we can have an attitude of listening: what do You want from me, Lord? What do You want me to do? Speak, Lord, your servant is listening.

It is that humble attitude that can achieve great things without stridence. It is that attitude that pleases the Lord, the attitude of humility, in which the Mother of God is a great example to seek inspiration. Mary calls herself "the slave of the Lord." And it is shown in total disposition to the will of God.

Jesus, I trust in You.

DONT TRY TO TAKE THE splinter out of anothers eye →

Remove the log from my own!

(SPIRITUAL way to IMPROVE EYESIGHT!)

13. Avoid gossiping

Sometimes we talk too much about others. We judge but we are not able to improve ourselves. We do not have the courage to examine ourselves, to be a bit more humble and to act accordingly.

We live in a world that is often fixed in the secondary and forgets the essential. And that same thing happens to us. Therefore Jesus tells us (Mt 7: 5):

"You're nothing but show-offs! First, take the log out of your own eye. Then you can see how to take the speck out of your friend's eye."

We all have areas to grow personally and spiritually. Prayer endeavors us to discover ourselves thanks to the communication with God. The Holy Mass is the highest place to understand where we are and what we have to do to move forward.

Talking too much about the others may cause us a certain distance from charity and little mercy towards people. Jesus, on the other hand, loves us and wants us humble and prudent. And it makes us realize, especially in our great mistakes, that we need more spiritual work to grow in love toward God.

Let's stop gossiping. Let's learn how to be silent longer. Let's learn to listen better to others and, in particular, to the will of God. Let us be truly wise and full of mercy.

Jesus, I trust in You.

14. Jesus' patience

Patience is one of the greatest virtues. If we look at the patience of Jesus towards us, we will realize that it is very great, that it is seventy times seven His forgiveness and welcoming embrace.

We must know how to forgive, to welcome spiritually, to understand, to be merciful as the Father. With a simple look and always with open arms. How does He do it with us?

Humanity is capable of the best and the worst. And not only do we need patience with others, but also with ourselves. Now, we always have the hope that Jesus does not get tired of us and He is always looking for how to make us react so we change our bad habits and transform them into holy habits.

Although we may be carrying many years of problems or difficulties, remember that the Gospel is full of curious and apparently incurable cases. A woman who had hemorrhages for 12 years (Mt 9, 20-22) or the sick man for 38 years (Jn 5, 1-9). In both cases there was a solution through Jesus.

There are difficulties in our way that seem impossible to overcome, that seem to last for a lifetime, but when it's really the time, Jesus gives us the necessary encouragement and tells us: be brave, your faith has saved you. Go in peace and do not sin anymore.

Jesus, I trust in You.

15. Dedicate time to friendship with Jesus

A priest explained once that we need to be right next to Jesus. That when we have the opportunity, we should dedicate time to Him. You do not have to go very far, you do not have to run. To allow the retreat of the soul is a necessary action.

Let's remember Martha and Mary. Martha is busy with many things. But Jesus values the attitude of Mary that accompanies Him from simplicity.

That is why Jesus warns us, as He did to Martha, that we are worried about many things in this world when there is only one really important thing, to be with the Lord. And from here, to be able to fill the world with light, good works and mercy. For this reason, what is said: "Whenever you did it for any of my people, no matter how unimportant they seemed, you did it for me."

To devote time to Jesus we're likely to take time out of our last priority. But it will be worth it. It is always worth being with Jesus, and what a glorious gift to be able to do it in the Eucharist!

Jesus, I trust in You.

16. Jesus' message: Do not be afraid

Sometimes we can become ghosts of our past. Jesus will repeat: do not be scared. Fear occasionally causes a lack of love. A lack of confidence. Therefore Jesus, in that 'do not be afraid' and in His petition to say "Jesus, I trust in You", wants to tell us that we are not alone. That He is very close.

But also, one of the greatest works of mercy is consoling sad and disconcerted, spending time with them, having the necessary patience and love. To pray if it is necessary, with them and for their sake.

We cannot go past those unfair situations we have around us. They are the Lazarus that we know and that awaits us, and we can not go past those Lazers that everyone has in their lives.

We, from our sense of understanding, can be a point of hope. Because Jesus, even though we are sinners, trusts us. Trusted Peter for the task of leading the Church even though He knew he would deny him three times and that he was not perfect.

Jesus trusts. He does not surrender. Generous heart to the maximum to the point of offering His own life. We are made in His image and likeness and He loves us. He has so much mercy towards us that He doesn't stop asking for our trust in return. Only trust and love, and a determined heart to love truthfully and generously.

Jesus, I trust in You.

17. Go to Mass with devotion

Sunday is the day of the Lord. Going to Mass should be something we have long awaited for. And if we can go there more days a week, let's go. And if we can be there every day, then better. The more the better. The Mass is the supreme prayer of thankfulness and Jesus is truly present. It is the greatest gift that Jesus has left us.

How can we forget that the most important thing is being given to us for free? And why does it often go unnoticed? It is the world that attracts us and wants our attention only for itself.

But who has given us life and prepares us a loving destiny, is not like a star that raises admiration, but on the contrary is the one who gives us what we need: peace, reconciliation and love to live with dignity. Even from poverty. From the austerity of the Lord's table, we are given the greatest wealth.

Mary, the Mother of God said: do what He tells you. Unfortunately, sometimes we do not follow her advice and we have to rectify. But who, being a father or a mother, won't wait with their arms open if their son humbly approaches looking for forgiveness?

Some times, people of good will profess devotion to the Virgin Mary or to the saints and forget, unconsciously, that both Mary and the saints have had the most important meeting point in God and in the Eucharist. And by seeing them, the saints of so many generations, we need to find Jesus.

Therefore, if Mary and the saints are aiming to approach us to Jesus, the perfect place where we find Jesus is in the Holy Mass. Let's go to Mass with joy, with a heart full of confidence, with the jewel that deserves a major event for our lives. And we can go there every day! If we listen carefully to the prayers, we will realize the blessing that they are and the importance they have.

In the Mass we live an enchanting, special mystery that we celebrate especially on Corpus Christi. Jesus is not a character of the past. He is alive and invites us to his table every day. Obviously if someone we admire calls us and invites us to have lunch, our hearts are filled with joy. Well, in this case, Jesus is the true God and the true man, who invites us! It's extraordinary!

Not only should we be happy but we should go to Mass with enthusiasm and this enthusiasm should be obvious, and we should convey it in our lives. And when someone asks us the reason of our happiness, we can say: every day I come across a person who offered their life for me and is still alive: Jesus of Nazareth.

Jesus, I trust in You.

Mary said "Do whatever He tells you"

He tells us to Love others & Forgive others

that's His will

Thy Will be Done!

Jesus invites us to His table everyday! most never go.

18. That technology doesn't make us lose love

Technology too often distorts us from what is important. Sometimes, the most important thing is to pay attention to the weakest, to those who need our attention and our loving smiles. Sometimes our selfishness wants to ignore true love. But there, in that mercy work, the Lord is hidden in the form of the helpless ones.

The parable of The rich man and Lazarus reminds us that we should not only be grateful but, according to our strength and possibilities, we have to listen to those who ask for our support and company.

We cannot fail in the key aspects of life. Mercy must always be present in our lives. Without works of mercy, without priority for mercy, our faith is not complete.

Jesus, I trust in You.

19. Do we love Jesus, or not?

In that time, Jesus said to his disciples: 21 "If you love me, you will do what I have said, and my Father will love you. I will also love you and show you what I am like." (John 14, 21)

Do we love Jesus? Do we follow the commandments? Or are there any commandments that we end up not wanting to fulfill? Do we really want to fulfill all the commandments? Or only those in our interest? Remember that Jesus remembers twice in the Gospel the words of the prophet Osees: what I want is love and not sacrifices. That is to say, Jesus does not demand great and extraordinary sacrifices, but to love Him constantly respecting the commandments.

If we love, it should not cost us sacrifices to seek how to fulfill God's will, because love and trust in Jesus allows us to transform our weak and sinful hearts into an honest, strong and loving heart.

Jesus acts not by calling the righteous, but the sinners. And it encourages us to trust Him every day to overcome our imperfections and our sins. Simply put, He wants us to trust Him and fulfill the commandments with love.

Jesus, I trust in You.

20. Ways to pray

There are many methods of prayer. The Catholic Charismatic Renewal has groups of community prayer where they combine songs, invocations to the Holy Spirit, prayers, reading a fragment of a Gospel, petitions...

The important thing is to pray with assiduity. There are thousands of simple devotions that help us: the Chaplet of the Divine Mercy, the Rosary, Angelus, visit the Blessed Sacrament... and among all these devotions, we must give priority to the Holy Mass.

Every day at least we can pray if we can not go to church. We can say the Lord's prayer, the Hail Mary, the Glory... We should pray as much as we can because the temptor wants to move us away from prayer. So, the only way to keep us safe is to create habits of prayer in the morning, noon, afternoon, night ...

Repeating certain prayers every day, and more or less at the same time, will help us keeping lit the lamp of faith.

Jesus, I trust in You.

Part Three: Understanding Mercy

21. The tempter wants us to move away from Jesus as their first objective

The Holy Mass is the source and climax of Christian life. That is why the tempter is quick to give excuses for not going to the Eucharist: they always say the same thing, it is heavy, it is long... But it is in Mass where everything begins. Where we remember where we come from. Where we deeply penetrate into the mystery. Where we live hope and, above all, where we find ourselves with our Lord Jesus Christ.

The love with which God loves us can be felt in the Mass. It is a communal prayer, where we celebrate our faith, where we review the most important passages of the Bible... That is to say, to go to Mass it is already trusting in God, it's telling Him: I am here, my Lord. I love You, I adore You. Also going to Mass is to confirm an action of thankfulness. The Eucharist means giving thanks, and Jesus always addressed that way to the Father. We also take pride in asking for forgiveness, we prepare to receive the holy mysteries. And we also pray for the intentions of the Church and the world and we are also capable of paying proper attention to what God expects from us.

Going to Mass with the utmost frequency, being constant in the great prayer of the Church, is a safe freeway in the improvement of our Christian life and also in our deepest happiness.

For this reason, due to the great importance of the Mass, we are encouraged at least once a year, to receive the sacrament of forgiveness, so we are better prepared to receive Jesus in communion. The confession, as the Papacy has repeatedly asked for, must be a place of mercy, and not a place of oppression. The confession is the sacrament where from humility we accept our sins and accept God's help to recover our dignity as people, a gift for us.

Jesus, I trust in You.

22. Faith, a gift that sometimes is not accepted

Faith is a gift that we sometimes do not want to accept. We prefer pride, our own beliefs, over accepting Jesus, the Humble of heart. Even if we pray a lot or if we do a lot of social work, we can fall into the vanity of considering ourselves better than others.

It is useless to continuously do good if we boast or if we consider ourselves better than the rest. Lack of humility may be the cause of scandal for third parties and their own downfall.

And the truth is that without modesty, there is no progress. Simple love shows us that God will not send us His message using power and pride. On the contrary, He did it from the most radical simplicity and from the most impressive humbleness.

Sometimes it's difficult for us to understand life and what happens on it. But if we seek justice and pray without fail, it is possible that we end up understanding that any hardship that touches us, properly approached, can be a blessing and a chance to be more humble, to understand our poverty and be a source of light for others. "Blessed are the poor in spirit" says Jesus in one of the Beatitudes.

Jesus, I trust in You.

23. People get salvation and forgiveness for their sins from God's deep love

The prayer of the Liturgy of the hours, which is highly recommended by the Church so that we can enter into the mystery of the love of God, offers us the celebration of two splendid hymns.

In Lauds' prayer you always say the Benedictus or Canticle of Zachary:

"Blessed be the Lord,
The God of Israel;
He has come to His people and set them free.

He has raised up for us a mighty Saviour,
Born of the house of His servant David.

Through His holy prophets He promised of old
That He would save us from our enemies,
From the hands of all who hate us.

He promised to show mercy to our fathers
And to remember His holy Covenant.

This was the oath He swore to our father Abraham:
To set us free from the hands of our enemies,

Free to worship Him without fear,
Holy and righteous in His sight
All the days of our life.

You, My child shall be called
The prophet of the Most High,
For you will go before the Lord to prepare His way,
To give his people knowledge of salvation
By the forgiveness of their sins.

In the tender compassion of our Lord
The dawn from on high shall break upon us,
to shine on those who dwell in darkness
And the shadow of death,
And to guide our feet into the way of peace."

On the other hand, in the Vespers, the song is the Magnificat, also a jewel of the Gospel of Saint Luke:

"My soul magnifies the Lord,
and my spirit rejoices in God my Savior;
Because He has regarded the lowliness of His handmaid.

For behold, henceforth all generations
shall call me blessed;
because He who is mighty has done great things for me.

Holy is His Name;
and His mercy is from generation to generation

on those who fear Him.

He has shown might with His arm,
He has scattered the proud in the conceit of their heart.
He has put down the mighty from their thrones,
and has exalted the lowly.
He has filled the hungry with good things,
and the rich he has sent away empty.

He has given help to Israel, His servant, mindful of His mercy
Even as He spoke to our father
to Abraham and to his posterity forever."

Let us look at this sentence: "He has scattered the proud in the conceit of their heart. He has put down the mighty from their thrones, and has exalted the lowly." The only way to improve is humility, make us small so that the love of Christ can grow within us.

Jesus, I trust in You.

24. Understand that after the cross comes the resurrection and the greatest life

There are times when we feel like inside us appears a kind of suffering. Our soul is sore. And suffering can exist in many different forms. Sometimes, we want to quickly throw it out the window. Sometimes we remind ourselves that Jesus died on the cross and he recommended us: whoever wants to be my disciple, should deny themselves and take their own cross to bear.

We all have different crosses to bear, some more bearable than others. And it is at the time of the cross, when we have to really prove if we are followers of Jesus or not.

By nature, the disciples flee from their crosses. They leave Jesus abandoned. We also do it sometimes. But with the help of the Holy Spirit, this reality can change and we can turn the burdensome moments into moments of Christian growth and hope.

After the cross of Jesus came the resurrection. Also after our daily crosses, the fruits will come if we are able to not throw the burden away and we know how to carry it with strength, patience and love.

Jesus wants love, not sacrifice. Therefore, making use of love in difficult times can make the difference. That is why prayer is so important. It is necessary to pray without fail. That is the reason why we can repeat in difficult times: Jesus, I trust in You.

25. How to beat temptation

God never fails. Trusting Jesus always makes our cross a more bearable and lightweight burden. On the other hand, human hopes are often weakened by facts that are not identical to our dreams or expectations.

The great trap of the evil is to tempt us as he did with Jesus in the desert. And if you do not stop it soon enough, it can lead to self-destruction.

Nature never forgives, years pass, time runs and if we do not know how to see the signs of time and we do not know how to live properly, we will be anticipating great disappointments. The rich man of the Gospel who repents only after having despised poor Lazarus, regrets not having had another attitude. But it was already too late. Even to warn his brother, who walked the same path and did not pay attention to the prophets.

Jesus says that it is more difficult for the rich to enter the kingdom of heaven than for a camel to go through the eye of a needle. It refers to the selfish wordly wealth, that does not think about others and finds joy in saying what the rich man said when he did not know what to do with so much money: 'I will throw the barns on the floor and I will build new ones...' But that very day he was called to the afterlife.

That is why the song of Mary, the Magnificat, is expressed thus: "He has scattered the proud in the conceit of their heart. He has put down the mighty from their thrones, and has exalted the lowly."

Humility is as important as prayer. Because a prayer without humility could be vain, scandalous, like that of the Pharisee who believes himself better than others. On the contrary, we must have a humble attitude because no matter how many virtues we have, we are always in danger of falling into an endless arrogance that leads us to the sin of vanity, a vanity that can scandalize and hurt.

Let us remember that God never fails. We are the ones who fail. And we need humility to cut the weeds off our garden, so we don't cloud the loving gaze of God that is actually the one that fills us up.

Let's use our weapons: let's attend Mass every day if we can or as much as possible, or if not at least on Sundays. Let's constantly pray as the saints did. Let's pray with eagerness or without it. Feeling comfort or not feeling it. It is the only remedy, the prayer, the communication with God. And we ask for forgiveness humbly and confidently. God accompanies us every day, every time and at all times.

Jesus, I trust in You.

26. The endless task of praying for others

Praying is very important and praying for the people we live with and the world can be decisive. Decisive because we can contemplate our poverty of spirit not knowing how to help them. Lord, how can I help that person? What do you want me to do?

Often we don't need to look far for the poor and the marginalization, we can often find them close by. Even in ourselves and in our environment. And it is when, again, we have to show if we are Christians and have faith, and especially if we are humble.

Jesus, who invites us to trust fully, invites us to pray for each other. We pray, therefore, for our relatives, for our friends, especially for those who need it most. Also for our enemies. And we also give thanks.

In times of great pressure and confusion the recipe is clear: humility, prayer and patience.

There is no other option left if we do not want to turn a difficult situation into an even more complicated one.

Prayer, like thin rain, is able to change the sterility of a situation into an opportunity to grow in love. We therefore take pride in praying for each other with simplicity. God already knows what we need before even asking for it.

(This novena prayer was recited every day by Padre Pio for all those who asked his prayers)

I. O my Jesus, You have said, 'Truly I say to you, ask and it will be given you, seek and you will find, knock and it will be opened to you.' Behold, I knock, I seek and ask for the grace of…

Our Father… Hail Mary… Glory be to the Father…
Sacred Heart of Jesus, I place all my trust in you.

II. O my Jesus, You have said, 'Truly I say to you, if you ask anything of the Father in my name, He will give it to you.' Behold, in Your name, I ask the Father for the grace of…

Our Father… Hail Mary… Glory be to the Father…
Sacred Heart of Jesus, I place all my trust in you.

III. O my Jesus, You have said, 'Truly I say to you, heaven and earth will pass away but my words will not pass away.' Encouraged by Your infallible words, I now ask for the grace of…

Our Father… Hail Mary… Glory be to the Father…
Sacred Heart of Jesus, I place all my trust in you.

O Sacred Heart of Jesus, for whom it is impossible not to have compassion on the afflicted, have pity on us poor sinners and grant us the grace which we ask of You, through the Sorrowful and Immaculate heart of Mary, Your tender mother and ours.

Hail, Holy Queen... St. Joseph, foster father of Jesus, pray for us.

Hail, holy Queen, Mother of mercy, our life, our sweetness and our hope.
To thee do we cry, poor banished children of Eve.
To thee do we send up our sighs, mourning and weeping in this valley of tears.
Turn then, most gracious Advocate, thine eyes of mercy towards us.
And after this, our exile, show unto us the blessed fruit of thy womb, Jesus.
O clement, O loving, O sweet Virgin Mary.

PRAYER OF PIETRELCINA:

Dear God, You generously blessed Your servant,
St. Pio of Pietrelcina, with the gifts of the Spirit.
You marked his body with the five wounds
of Christ Crucified, as a powerful witness
to the saving Passion and Death of Your Son.

Hail, Purest Mary! Conceived without sin!

Let's trust. Let us pray every day without failing.

Jesus, I trust in You.

27. The temptations have one purpose: to separate us from the love of God

The tempter always seeks to separate us from Jesus. We are tempted in a thousand small things so we leave humility and fall into arrogance. The temptations are clear or blurry but usually they always come in the least expected moments or moments of weakness. Temptations of all kinds, even in the midst of good works.

For example, a prayer made with vanity can lead us to sin easily. A work of mercy made with pride can lose all value and cause pain and scandal.

Therefore, we need lots of prayer and lots of humility to be faithful. And since the tempter knows that we need a lot of prayer, they look for the way to get us away from prayer, or what is the same, to get us away from God.

So, it is not enough to go with the flow. In a world where the devil has managed to convince everybody that he does not exist, it is when he can work with more subtlety, more cleverly. And people often do not realize that the constant work of the devil is this, guide us towards pride so we fall into the temptation in one way or another instead of being poor in spirit, which is the first Beatitude.

The only way to fight is to do it with the weapons of faith. Mass as frequent as possible, if we can go every day, what a privilege! And confess without fear and whenever it is needed at least once a year. With these two big weapons plus personal or communal prayer, we can always keep going and at least get up quickly if we have fallen.

The simple brief prayers: "Jesus, I trust in You", "Come, Holy Spirit and fill our hearts" can be the antidote in difficult times. And also the sincere question to God: "Lord, what do you want me to do?" And for those who can, the Rosary is the greatest weapon. St. Pius de Pietrelcina said it many times during the day, reviewing the different mysteries. He was tempted but with the help of the Virgin Mary, he always won. We can learn from him.

Praying humbly is the best guarantee.

Jesus, I trust in You.

28. Pray for peace and love in the family

Peace starts at home. Peace to you, repeated Jesus resurrected. Peace is a gift. Peace in families, pray for those who are our relatives and for peace is very necessary today.

The tempter knows that one of the most important places where he can cause great damage is within families. Causing division, doubts, verbal or physical violence...

And it is more necessary than ever to pray for peace in our family. Only in times of peace there is healthy progress in all fields. Especially in love.
Because there is peace there must be humility and forgiveness. And for them to present themselves to us, it is important to pray for each other. Pray for our relatives, thanking all the good things they have given us.

The destruction of the family is the destruction of society. That is why it is so basic to pray for the family, for our families and for the world, so that we can live in peace and love.

Without a doubt, going to church with the family can be a great blessing and source of union. Praying with your family can be another great blessing!

Jesus, I trust in You.

29. Why pray for vocations

Jesus asked us Christians to ask the owner of the fields new vocations. Jesus asked us for it. The reason is simple The tempter works to make vocations become lost in the consecrated life and to overwhelm the existing vocations. Hence it makes sense to pray for vocations in religious life and also to pray for the consecrated ones.

Spiritual combat is not easy in this world. And less for those who want to do good and want to consecrate themselves to God being faithful. There are many temptations of all kinds that affect or may affect priests, monks or religious people in general. Among the crowd: doubts of faith, pride, envy, sadness, etc. All in all to create confusion and push people into sin.

That is why it is so important to remember the priests and the religious, pray for new vocations and pray so that those existing can be firm in faith and attentive to charity.

The consecrated are the servers. They leave everything to offer themselves to God and to others. But in a technological world marked by advertising impacts that often defend interests other than charity, it is necessary and imperative to value and pray for vocations. So the Almighty with the intervention of the Blessed Virgin Mary, can make consecrated or aspiring, good and holy examples of Christian life.

We leave the destructive criticisms and pray for the consecrated ones, especially those who have more responsibility. We trust Jesus, who wants to send his mercy towards them so that they can expand.

We do not abandon our prayers, this unity with God, so that it can attend today's disciples in their moments of trial and difficulty.

Jesus, I trust in You.

30. To do good and live a saintly life affects those near us and the whole world

The kindness that we can create thanks to the love of God that we receive, all works of mercy, all patience, all the fruits of love, translate into an increase of hope and quality of life, especially in our side, but also affects the whole society.

We do not know to what extent our good works will affect and make changes, and we do not have to know it either. What is important, after all, is to do good without seeking recognition, being humble and always remembering that God first loved us, that he has given us life. So, as Saint Paul recommends, we always live happy in the Lord and do good.

Jesus came to bring the commandments to their peak. Not that the ten commandments given to Moses were not fulfilled, but to take them a little further. In other words, do not settle for not killing, but being defenders of life and helping those who suffer living. Do not settle for not lying, but for being seekers of peace and justice.

Do not settle for not committing adultery, but for not looking at someone else with desire to have them... And so on. Blessings and the sermon on the mountain

ospel chapters from 5 to 7) do not devalue
iments but culminate the concept of love
achings of Jesus.

But it is clear that not in all stages of faith there is enough maturity to understand how God loves us. There is some inability to lead a fairly straightforward life.

If we understood how God loves us, only because of gratitude we would practically give life in order not to defraud Him. However, Jesus, the creator of all good, aware of our weak reality, encouraged Santa Faustina to propagate devotion to Divine Mercy, to frequently say "Jesus, I trust in You" and to pray the Chaplet so that faith could mature in people in such a way that Jesus himself was no longer seen in the mystery of faith as a distant person, but as one who is always present in the Tabernacle and as the one who invites us every day to Mass and is always present right beside us.

Jesus tells us: come to me, all who are tired and afflicted, and I will make you rest.

There is nothing impossible for Jesus. In the Gospel we have proof of healings after many years and surely that already the majority would think those patients had nothing to do anymore. But Jesus does not rule anyone, Jesus gives us the hand not to sink. Jesus is alive.

Gradually maturing our faith can take time. But let's not be discouraged. Jesus wants to quench our thirst with his infinite mercy. The Father, the Son and the Holy Spirit, the Holy Trinity, do not cease in their merciful love because just as it happens with the prodigal son, we return from God, again, with renewed strength. The Trinity always waits for us with open arms and rejoices over a sinner who converts.

Jesus, I trust in You.

Fourth part: Be a part of mercy

31. To each setback, a greater door to trust in Jesus

In life, we stumble upon lots of setbacks on a daily basis. Events that go against how we predict them. But we are also artificers, sometimes, of attitudes that go against the love of God towards us.

In this kind of occasions, we must remember the centrality of Jesus' message, that we can experience to the maximum at Holy Mass. For this reason, going to the mass with as much frequency as we can, makes us see things from a more panoramic and not that wordly view.

In Mass Jesus is really present. We can ask for forgiveness, express how thankful we are, worship God, pray for the needs of the world, join in communion with so many people who approach the table of the Lord to live the mystery of the resurrection.

Jesus is alive. He is not some historical character of the past. Jesus looks at us with tenderness and asks for us to put our trust in Him. That His yoke is soft and His load, lightweight. To verify this, in the Mass we listen to the

Word of God, think about it and pray together in community to always remember that the love of God follows us every day.

Jesus, I trust in You.

32. Live with the essential and bring it to fullness

Jesus went beyond the Old Testament, He wanted to keep the essential and bring it to fullness.

Jesus at the Sermon on the Mount (Gospel of St. Matthew chapter 5, 17-20) tells us:
17 Don't suppose that I came to do away with the Law and the Prophets.
 I did not come to do away with them, but to give them their full meaning. 18 Heaven and earth may disappear. But I promise you that not even a period or comma will ever disappear from the Law. Everything written in it must happen.

19 If you reject even the least important command in the Law and teach others to do the same, you will be the least important person in the kingdom of heaven. But if you obey and teach others its commands, you will have an important place in the kingdom. 20 You must obey God's commands better than the Pharisees and the teachers of the Law obey them. If you don't, I promise you that you will never get into the kingdom of heaven.

Jesus, therefore, does not abolish the 10 commandments. Not only does He ask for us to love God over all things, but to do it with all our heart, with all our soul, with all our thoughts and all our strength (Matthew 12:30).

Not only does He ask for us not to say the name of God in vain, but warns us that we should always know how to separate for God what is from God and for the Caesar what is the Caesar's.

Not only does He ask for us to sanctify the festivities, but to live them alongside Him in the Eucharist and then apply them into our charity towards others.

Not only does He ask for us to honor our father and mother, but also to love our enemies.

Not only does He ask for us not to kill, but to fight for life, to love the weakest: the sick, the marginalized, the prisoners, the children, the underprivileged, the disabled...

Not only does He ask for us not to do sinful actions, but also to respect every human being.

Not only does He asks for us not to steal, but to contribute to the common benefit by putting our talents at service with generosity.

Not only does He ask for us not to commit perjury or to tell lies, but to be bearers of truth and work for the sake of justice as we are told in the Beatitudes.

Not only does He ask for us not to consent to impure thoughts or desires, but rather encourages us to be perfect as the Father is.

And not only does He ask for us not to desire other's possessions, but to put at service our own possessions without selfishness.

Therefore, Jesus is demanding of the essential but rejects the secondary needs. Therefore, He heals on Saturday, he puts people first. And He encourages us not to put heavy senseless burdens on others' shoulders.

Jesus is demanding because he knows that we can do many things for our world. We have the ability to love. And God knows that we will be able to do very well if we trust Him.

Jesus, I trust in You.

33. Humility is necessary when we do good

One of the greatest temptations when we fulfill the commandments of Jesus is to think that we are doing something extraordinary. It is a temptation that can come to us and that we must quickly and humbly put aside. Because the pride that comes from a perfect life can be worse than an ordinary life without pride.

In the Gospel of the Sermon on the Mount, Jesus warns us severely not to be hypocrites, not to do what we have to do simply to show off or to receive recognition from others.

That's why Jesus tells us that when we fast, when we give alms or when we pray, three penitent and good actions, we should always do it with discretion and not to seek fame, prestige, power or admiration.

Jesus asks for humility from us, so that He can be the one who values what we do, if not, he tells us that we already have the reward. For this reason, we must always seek to have Jesus' feelings and often go to the sacraments, to remember that we are weak and that without Jesus, we can not do anything.

Jesus, I trust in You.

34. John Baptist shows us Jesus and how to make him enter our lives

John Baptist, considered by Jesus Himself as the greatest of the prophets, accomplishes a special mission, baptizing with water and preparing the ways of the Lord. Jesus Himself humbly asked to be baptized, but John said that he was not even worthy to untie His shoes.

Jesus does not want privileges, He walks the world fulfilling the law and bringing it to fullness. John warns the people that he only baptizes them with water, clamouring for the conversion. Thus, when we prepare to receive Jesus, we must have this attitude, the attitude of conversion, of wanting to be with Jesus well-prepared and willing to receive Him and then be able to do as many works of mercy as Jesus asks us to do.

John had to decrease so Jesus could grew up. So we have to diminish our sins and our unloving attitudes, so that the temple of the Holy Spirit may grow inside us and Jesus Himself can stay there.

God trusts us. He trusted John the Baptist to prepare the paths. And He trust us too, because with our example of life and according to our talents we prepare the ways so that many can approach Jesus, to know and to experiment this experience of unconditional love that He offers us.

Each one of us has a series of talents, and we must cultivate them with the necessary humility and constancy. Yes, humility and perseverance are our guardians. Without humility the talents do not bear any fruit because it is eaten by pride. Without constancy the talents can not be able to male the fruit grow, because they are not cultivated enough to do so.

Therefore, we undermine all that is bad in our lives and we grow loving habits, especially devotion to the Holy Mass, which can be better everyday, since it will set up a spirit of love and charity that will make us able to do good works constantly.

Jesus, I trust in You.

35. All saints agree with the devotion to the Mass

There are many devotions: the Rosary, the Chaplet of the Divine Mercy, the Lauds, Vespers, Novenas... But there is no more important devotion than the sacrament of the Eucharist. The Holy Mass is the source of all holiness, a privileged place where saints have lived, experimented and matured their faith. They may have been saints who have done an extraordinary social work, such as Mother Teresa of Calcutta, but they all agree in a special devotion to the Holy Mass.

Mother Teresa of Calcutta said: "Mass is the spiritual food that sustains me and without which I could not live a single day or a single hour of my life."

All saints of all time and with all kinds of charisma see in the Eucharist the food of eternal life and the source of energy they need to properly love. Because in the Eucharist Jesus becomes present. We are in community with Jesus and this is so extraordinary that Saint Teresa of Calcutta emphasizes the Mass as the spiritual food that keeps us going.

St John Baptist de la Salle would say: "Who works manually and has to deal with temporary and external matters all day, must make the Holy Mass their first concern and action." Therefore, the Mass is and should be as frequent as possible. Because it is a source of joy, love and holiness.

Jesus, I trust in You.

36. Effort to enter through the narrow door

In two Gospels we are talking about the narrow door, in Matthew and Luke. In Matthew, in the framework of the Sermon on the Mount, Jesus remarks: 13 "Enter through the narrow gate. For wide is the gate and broad is the road that leads to destruction, and many enter through it. 14 But small is the gate and narrow the road that leads to life, and only a few find it."

It seems like a very hard message that raises a difficult Christianity, full of privations. But in fact, Jesus himself suffers at times having passed through the narrow door and fulfilling the will of the Father. It is a warning, a warning that reminds us of all those times when pride wants to make us forget about God and about the others.

Jesus tells us about effort. How many times have we seen athletes or actors and actresses, who, after great efforts to reach the summit, fall through the wide door of perdition?

How many times do we, as a result of the pride that is sometimes born inside us, enter the wide door of perdition after good days when we have been going through the narrow gate?

Jesus, therefore, tells us that temptations are multiple and the straight path and holiness are completely discreet. In the Gospel of Saint Luke (13, 24) Jesus says: 24 "Do all you can to go in by the narrow door! A lot of people will try to get in, but will not be able to."

Effort sometimes causes pain, and the faithful and constant effort can cause temptations of all kinds: jealousy, bitterness, envy, sadness, desire to abandon, dullness... All tempting feelings because we fall into the great temptation of the wide door, which apparently should give us happiness, but that's just a mirage.

This is why it is so important to attend Mass, because there we have the consolation of the Scriptures, the gift of God's love that renews our joy and our hope. Jesus tells us in the Mass that we should not be afraid, that He is benevolent and humble of heart. And Saint Paul will tell us: be happy, always happy in the Lord.

In the Mass we are in community and we can pray for each other and for the needs of the world. And Jesus is with us to give us strength so the effort is neither so harsh nor sterile.

Jesus is given to us in the Mass, which is a narrow door that many forget. But the Mass, the source of all holiness and joy, the sacrament that sanctifies, gives us what can not give the broad door of perdition: the water that sinks, Jesus himself that lives and rises.

Jesus, I trust in You.

37. You can tell what they are by what they do

There are important Gospels to understand the attitude we must have and how to bear fruit. As a graft of Jesus and having pulled up the weeds of bad habits and sins, we can someday bear fruit.

In the Gospel of Matthew (7, 15-20), Jesus tells us:

15 >>Watch out for false prophets! They dress up like sheep, but inside they are wolves who have come to attack you. 16 You can tell what they are by what they do. No one picks grapes or figs from thornbushes.
17 A good tree produces good fruit, and a bad tree produces bad fruit. 18 A good tree cannot produce bad fruit, and a bad tree cannot produce good fruit. 19 Every tree that produces bad fruit will be chopped down and burned.
20 You can tell who the false prophets are by their deeds.<<

Jesus, therefore, tells us how we can know people to a higher extent and how we can better understand ourselves. The patience of Jesus is big. As the psalmist tells us: He is the Lord God He is merciful and very patient with His people. He shows great love, and He can

But in life, if we do not rectify and do not bear precisely us who can end up being hurt. If we do not fulfill our duties, we are the ones who are not bearing the fruit that our talents must produce.

In the Parable of the Talents, who had less talents was afraid of losing them so they kept them safe. On the other hand, those who had more, worked their talents and produced twice.

That is the reason Jesus says "Do not be afraid", because Jesus does not ask that we bear fruit from our weak spots, but he commands us to bear fruit from our talents, from those things God has made special in every one of us and that allow us to help others in an unique way.

This is where the key is: to bear fruit and make our talents work. Yes, our talents are cut off every time we sin, every time we say no to Jesus and yes to any bad habit. But Jesus tells us: do not be afraid, you are much more important than any birds.

Because God loves us, He does not want us to be bitter. He wants us to bear fruit in our vocation.

For this reason, the Church and the world are so diverse, full of different vocations and different charisma; but the Spirit is the one that always unites us in the Lord and invites us to the Mass to share together the joy of overcoming sin and live the resurrection.

Jesus, I trust in You.

38. The priority of the daily Mass, direct meeting with Jesus

In the countries with a deeply rooted Christian presence, we are fortunate enough to have options to go to Mass, both in the morning and at night on weekdays or at least once a day in most parishes. In an increasingly flexible working environment, this can give us an extraordinary opportunity to go to Mass for many days and not just holidays.

Fortunately, there are parishes with one or two daily masses. And other parishes, larger, with up to six daily masses in some capitals. This gives us a spectacular range of options to go share the Lord's Table. It gives us the opportunity to feel the consolation of eternal love. The strength to keep going. The teaching of biblical texts to improve our knowledge of ourselves.

Holy Mass is not only a privileged space, but it is the great space where most other sacraments are received. And it is the way Jesus commanded His disciples to do it. Throughout the year we have celebrations of all kinds and varieties. For example, on Friday after Corpus Christi, we celebrate the feast of the Sacred Heart of Jesus and the day after the feast of the Sacred Heart of Mary.

Almost every day we have holy holidays, which are an example of Christian virtues and various charisms, but always of unconditional and faithful love towards the Lord.

And in every Mass we always have a multitude of messages and prayers that seek communion, love, peace, solidarity, unity... Always in the company of Jesus, who becomes present inside us to console us, to offer every part of Himself to us, to say: I am here with you and I will always be.

The Mass is an awesome gift. We have already commented it on this book. And if we have to prioritize between a prayer and the Mass, we should always opt for the Mass, this supreme prayer where we experience the joy and happiness of love embodied in the risen Jesus.

Jesus, I trust in You.

39. Confidence, the medicine of the soul

When we are in painful moments or we feel inner sadness, it is very important to repeat the prayer "Jesus, I trust in You." Confidence radically changes a sad expression into a brave smile. We feel the embrace of God around us as in the Prodigal Son. God is always ready to give us comfort, to embrace us, to love us so deeply that there is no place in our hearts for sadness.

Even so, God also leaves in people's hands the ability to make that this love that He has given us, can also be manifested through us. We, especially those who feel the love of God in us, are the ones who have to transmit this love in deeds and have to console. And if we do not know how to do it, we must go humbly to the Lord and raise our doubts and our poverty. Thus, God that is infinite abundance, will nurture us with the power and food of eternal life so, according to our talents, we can be able to give love to others or know how to act at all times.

Self-sufficiency or thinking we are superior or perfect beings is very dangerous. Therefore, we must feel poor in spirit and always lacking in this love and gifts that the Holy Spirit always gives us, to move forward in the love towards others, in the progress to love our neighbour.

The medicine of the soul is confidence. Trust Jesus, who waits for our prayer to be able to console us and guide us through the Holy Spirit.

There is no doubt that in life we will go through dark times. But if we pray from poverty, darkness will become light.

Jesus, I trust in You.

Part five: Advancing in mercy

40. You always move forward, although it may not seem obvious, from humility and sincere search for God and justice

Sometimes, time and years pass, and there seems to be no progress in our spiritual life. It seems we're feeling the same and repeating our successes and our mistakes. Or that they get even worse.

Jesus, who loves us, understands our situations and asks from us the commitment to love and do everything possible to improve. Praying to God from the bottom of the heart and with all possible humility makes that situations that seem at a standstill can be one day resolved very quickly.

For this reason, we can not be discouraged by the mistakes that we make. On the contrary, we must always stand up to Jesus as told in the Gospel of St Matthew (chapter 14, verses 22 to 33):
22 Right away, Jesus made his disciples get into a boat and start back across the lake.

But he stayed until he had sent the crowds away. 23 Then he went up on a mountain where he could be alone and pray. Later that evening, he was still there.

24 By this time the boat was a long way from the shore. It was going against the wind and was being tossed around by the waves. 25 A little while before morning, Jesus came walking on the water toward his disciples. 26 When they saw him, they thought he was a ghost. They were terrified and started screaming.

27 At once, Jesus said to them, "Don't worry! I am Jesus. Don't be afraid."

28 Peter replied, "Lord, if it is really you, tell me to come to you on the water."

29 "Come on!" Jesus said. Peter then got out of the boat and started walking on the water toward him.

30 But when Peter saw how strong the wind was, he was afraid and started sinking. "Save me, Lord!" he shouted.

31 Right away, Jesus reached out his hand. He helped Peter up and said, "You surely don't have much faith. Why do you doubt?"

32 When Jesus and Peter got into the boat, the wind died down. 33 The men in the boat worshiped Jesus and said, "You really are the Son of God!"

If Peter fell, was afraid and felt the reproach of Jesus "You surely don't have much faith. Why do you doubt?" It may someday be our turn to experience fear and fall. But Jesus tells us: Be brave, do not be afraid. And He will extend His hand to grab us and save us from the cliff and bring us back the dignity of the Children of God. Humbly, we must accept His help, confess and do our utmost to be faithful again by renewing our commitment to God.

Jesus, I trust in You.

41. Faith just as a mustard seed and its cultivation

Every plant must be watered if we want to make it grow. Also our faith, if we want it to grow, we must celebrate it and live it. The prayer and especially the Holy Mass are the ideal surroundings to make faith grow, to pray humbly and to say: Jesus, I trust in You. Then there will be the good works that we will offer the world according to the advice of the Eucharist.

In the Gospel of Matthew, Mark and Luke, Jesus tells us this parable that we are now extracting from the Gospel of Matthew (13, 31-32):

31 Jesus told them another story:
The kingdom of heaven is like what happens when a farmer plants a mustard seed in a field. 32 Although it is the smallest of all seeds, it grows larger than any garden plant and becomes a tree. Birds even come and nest on its branches.

Therefore, however little our faith is, if we cultivate it with certainty, it will not only grow, but it may even become the help and consolation to many others.

Thus, the recipe is very simple: humility and perseverance in the experience of our faith, which translates in attending Holy Mass as much as we can to honor God, to meet Risen Jesus and to receive the strength of the Holy Spirit, to pray with simplicity with as much fervor as possible and by serving and loving others as Jesus loves us.

Jesus, I trust in You.

42. Jesus' response to temptations

The devil tempts Jesus in a moment of human weakness. Jesus is hungry and thirsty because He is in the desert. We are also tempted at moments of weakness. The Prince of lies opens the wide door every time he sees the opportunity, for the Christian to enter and fall into the trap.

But the answers of Jesus must stimulate us not to give up and the example of the saints must make us live with hope. Battling against temptation does not have to make us end up defeated.

In the temptations we see three levels. At the first level people want pleasures. Jesus reminds the tempter that man does not live by bread alone.

The second level is the ambition of power, and the last one the ambition of recognition.

At first, especially in moments of human weakness, sadness, depression, we seek consolation in food or in human pleasures. Then, covered by primary needs, the tempter drives us towards the path of power, but Jesus reminds us that we can not tempt the Lord. Power, therefore, is a means of service, not a means of opression.

Finally, if we already have the primary needs resolved and certain status in the spirit of service, the devil tempt us into looking for recognition or hoping for it. Instead, Jesus encourages us to consider ourselves poor and humble in heart, useless servants, but loved by God. And only to worship God. And do not expect us to be worshiped.

Jesus is blunt in His answers to the evil and His example must be useful to us so we keep firm and resolute when temptation appears.

Thus, in the fight against temptations there are three great virtues and a weapon. The virtues are humility, purity and obedience. And the weapon is prayer, especially the sacraments. Those are the virtues of Mary, the mother of God, and that is why so many saints have come to holiness, putting themselves under the affiliation of Mary and learning from the Mother of God, who loves us so much and lived humility, purity and obedience to the maximum degree. Therefore, to Jesus, through Mary.

Temptations are and will always be present in our lives. St. Pius de Pietrelcina fought against the temptations with the Rosary. If necessary, he prayed many times during the day in order not to succumb to numerous temptations that were placed before him. But his fidelity, his humility and its purity, similar to that of Mary, triumphed and continues to triumph in Heaven doing good on Earth, as the great Holy Teresa of the Infant Jesus also said.

Against temptations, humility. And if we fall, in order to rise up, humility. Humility is the first and most necessary virtue, totally opposed to the pride of the Devil.

Jesus, I trust in You.

43. Offerings of suffering for those in need

A great highway towards holiness is to offer our daily sufferings for those who suffer or need spiritual healing. Abstaining from evil, reject the unworthy and offer this love to God for the sake of those who need it the most bears great fruit.

Sometimes we may be needed by lots of people and we have the option of making a more complete prayer to God, lovingly offering our daily setbacks to God and a positive intention towards a person who is going through something difficult.

Every day, whether we like it or not, we are almost certainly assaulted by painful moments, which we can offer in a special way for intentions and people who need our offerings.

Jesus, I trust in You.

44. Aridity for our sake

When we have spent some time fulfilling the will of God and celebrating the sacraments with fervor, aridity is likely to arise. A time when we do not feel anything when we celebrate and live the sacraments. We are living in some kind of dark night without any apparent reason.

The aridity, therefore, is a test of faith or a state that helps us purify our trust in God and our fidelity to Him. It does not happen to everyone, but it is true that many people go through this state.

Even so, if we know how to remain faithful, we can continue to walk on fertile land. And it will bear great fruit.

Jesus, I trust in You.

45. The communion of the saints and their help

There are times when we can feel helpless, where it seems that instead of doing the good we would like to do, we do all the bad we are trying to avoid. Well, at this kind of times, it may be very interesting asking for the intercession of the saints and good people we have known but who are no longer with us here on Earth.

Since we believe in the communion of the saints, we believe that they pass us Heaven by doing good on Earth. So much so, that their intercession helps us to get up and return to God's side more strongly.

We always need humility to ask for help and we must always do this from a simple attitude. We can not be arrogant, as Christians, we must keep humble, simple, and ask the help of all those saints who accompany us with their intercession.

Our patron or patroness saint will surely be a faithful intercessor. But since God has wanted to give us freedom and become bearers of love, we must also, humbly, on our own initiative, ask for His help. Surely, it will be very effective.

Jesus, I trust in You.

46. Mary, full of grace

Being in God's grace is an extraordinary state since we are prepared for the greatest, to receive Jesus. Living in the grace of God and participating in the Eucharist is an awesome act.

Mary is full of grace. How much can we learn from the Virgin Mary, help for the Christians and refuge of sinners? How much love continues to shed so many and so many people who cite their prayer every day "now and at the time of our death"?

Mary is the example of being in grace always. We can, because of our unfaithfulness, momentarily lose grace. But if we feel deep down we're Mary's children and pray to the Virgin Mary, we will feel that she expects us to be eager to receive forgiveness. Because God loves us and this great love comparable to that of parents towards their children, that always makes us find healing again and be once again in God's grace.

The saying goes that every day is holy and good for those who live in the grace of God. And being in grace is the best that can happen to us and what we have to desire to maintain, with the utmost loyalty and with maximum respect. Grace is a great gift of God. We have to value it.

Jesus, I trust in You.

47. Invoking the Holy Spirit

"Come Holy Spirit and fill my heart." "Come Holy Spirit and fill our hearts." This request to the Holy Spirit is a very good prayer. Like the one of "Jesus, I trust in You", because we are asking for the presence of God in us and we are trusting in the strength God brings us.

Our world, in general, has forgotten God. And, unfortunately, many Christians sometimes forget God, so it is important to have an arsenal of short or powerful prayers for saying at certain times of the day, because they will give us that love's strength we need so much.

God wants us to pray. The memory of God must manifest Him with humility and simplicity. And doing so, we can revive strongly this love that wants to stay deep down inside us.

St. Paul shows us clearly in the first letter addressed to the Corinthians (3, 16-17): 16 All of you surely know that you are God's temple and that his Spirit lives in you. 17 Together you are God's holy temple, and God will destroy anyone who destroys his temple.

Therefore, when we gravely sin we can destroy the temple of God and therefore, destroy ourselves. Only the mercy of God can lift us through the sacrament of reconciliation and, therefore, it is so important to pray without fail, not to fall into grave sin and in case of doing it, to not persist and to rectify quickly. Because, otherwise, living without the love of God leads us to self-destruction.

Thus, it is important that we live for the Lord, facing Him and always paying close attention to His instruments of love and His sacraments. Especially, if we can go to Mass every day or very often, a lot better, it is the supreme prayer in which the fact of receiving the Holy Spirit becomes even more powerful.

Come, Holy Spirit, and fill my heart.

Prayer to the Holy Spirit
From Cardinal Verdier:

Oh Holy Spirit,
Love of the Father, and of the Son,

Inspire me always
what I should think,
what I should say,
how should I say it,

when should I keep silent,
how should I act,

what should I do for the glory of God
good for souls and my own sanctification.

Holy Spirit,
give me acuteness to understand,
ability to retain,
method and faculty to learn,
subtlety to interpret,
grace and efficiency to speak.

Give me success at the beginning,
direction to progress,
and perfection at the end.

Amen.

Jesus, I trust in You.

48. Prayer renews us internally

Our exterior may seem the same. In fact, it is difficult to know a person just by seeing them. Appearances can deceive. Even internally, we can change. And this renovation has a privileged place when we pray.

The prayer of each day and especially the holy Mass give us the peace we desire as well as strength of spirit to face the challenges of our lives. Sometimes inside we feel like we are in a fight, it is a spiritual struggle, and as such, we can only overcome it by using prayer.

Sometimes it is hard to pray, but it is in prayer, it is in this communication with God, where we can truly transform our interior in such a way that is no longer us who live, but the very Jesus living within us.

Pray, pray, pray. Pray on every occasion Jesus says, be aware of human weakness. We pray because, despite our spirit is devoted, flesh is weak. Let us pray so that we can live in the grace of God, feeling this love that awaits us, that encourages us to be better and better, to know how to love better.

Praying is essential. If a Christian does not pray, he automatically stops being a Christian. The world and the

Devil want to get us away from prayer, because they know that to fall into temptation, the more we leave our prayers, the stronger the fall can be.

Therefore, let's pray without fail, let's quickly get up whenever we fall and keep the heart open to God to pray for each other, to love God with all the heart and all the strength, because He gave His life for us, to make us live forever.

Holy Mass, a privileged place for God's love towards us, should always be our priority prayer, and we should make of it the great event of our lives. Because it is at Mass where the source of love that does not end springs up.

Jesus, I trust in You.

49. What did Jesus do at moments of maximum pressure?

In the Gospel of Matthew 14, 13-21, we find ourselves with a situation of maximum pressure where circumstances seem to overcome human forces. The situation arises after a very hard fact, John has been murdered in the hands of Herod and when Jesus discovers it, goes to the desert, probably to pray and regain calmness.

But when Jesus needs more peace, the crowd follows Him. Jesus, instead of worrying and make the people leave, sympathizes and heals the sick. When it ends, after the tiredness of the day, the disciples warn Jesus that they will not be able to attend the crowd, and it would be good to recommend them to go to the nearest villages to buy some food.

Jesus, however, says to the disciples: "You do not need to leave, give them something to eat yourselves". The disciples complain to Jesus about the little supply of what they have, only five breads and two fish, but here is the reaction of Jesus: He commands the crowd to sit down and glancing to the sky, He pronounces a blessing and breaks the bread into pieces to give them to the people.

So Jesus, instead of being angry, thanks God for what He has and breaks the bread. It's a great lesson and the result can not be better, there is still plenty to eat.

In our lives, in many occasions, we feel tired and as we could not face the challenges that our lives are put under. We feel no energy, and lacking any resources. But Jesus teaches us the way: to approach Him, to thank for what we have, although it may seem insufficient to us. And He recommends breaking the bread, that is, sharing whatever we have.

This is a Gospel that we will have to apply by force in our lives, since our weaknesses sometimes will make us say: Lord, what do You want me to do to face this situation? We must put our trust in God and remember the steps of Jesus' love: to thank Jesus, to trust in Jesus and to share what we have although we may feel it is not much, that is, to share our talents the best we can. By doing so, the results will be impressive even if the means are scarce, because for God nothing is impossible.

Jesus, I trust in You.

50. Mary, the perfect model to walk towards holiness

The well-known exorcist from the Vatican, P.Gabriele Amorth (1925-2016) explains how the Devil once explained to him why the virtues of the Virgin Mary hurt the evil one the most. First of all, because she is the most humble of all creatures. Contrary to the Devil, who is the most arrogant amongst them all.

Second, Mary is the purest of all creatures. While the Devil is the dirtier. And, finally, Mary is the most obedient to God of all creatures, while the Devil is rebellious.

Thus, this easily, we realize the wide door of pride, dirt and rebellion. This is the easiest way to take. Instead, being humble, pure and obedient is a lot harder.

We have often spoken of humility, and in Mary we find humility personified.

Humility, purity, obedience. Three words that bear the love, fidelity, and hope of faith. Light to the world.
So, if we want to transform our heart and look inside Mary's heart, we must have humility first, learn to

recognize our sins and ask for God's help through confession, to rise and live in grace.

And then, feed yourself with the maximum frequency of Holy Mass, to have the constant energy and strength to do the works of mercy that we have to do in our life.

Thus, with the power of the sacraments and with prayers such as the Angelus, the rosary or the Chaplet of the Divine Mercy, we will move forward, with real hope, towards the love and feelings that God expects us to have within. Being carriers of peace and hope wherever we go.

We can say: thanks, my Lord, for Your love. Thank You for the life, for the peace and the regeneration that we feel thanks to You. Come, Holy Spirit, and fill our hearts.

Jesus, I trust in You.

Part six: Examples of mercy

51. Saint John Bosco, holiness is joy

Why did St. John Bosco say that sanctity is joy if we sometimes have to bear heavy crosses? He said this, because among all the options to live according to our current state, Jesus' option is the one that gives us joy and hope.

St John Bosco loved young people and made them see that the most attractive proposal to live is the proposal of Jesus' love. And living this proposal should make us happy because, in all possible ways, it will make us live in a more complete and more satisfactory way.

You can not picture holiness like living in bitterness and sadness. But on the contrary, it should be pictured as a mystery of love, so great that when communicating it, especially with the testimony, it can bring joy and hope wherever we go.

The commandments are not to destroy the person who follows them, but to bring that person to fullness. St John

Bosco, who helped many young people, made them see that we can all be holy and that we should, from the joy of being Christian, love the world with kindness and serenity, to comfort the sad and release the captives from the slavery of bad habits.

Prayer is the great stimulant. Going to Mass is to complete the steps towards joy, so that it can be shared when you leave.

St John Bosco, we ask you to intercede for us, to see the beauty and joy of living as Christians.

Jesus, I trust in You.

52. Saint Josemaría Escrivá, sanctity in the state of life, in our vocation, in our ordinary daily life

It appears in the Gospel (Matthew 5: 48) and St. Josemaría Escrivá promoted it. We must look for the sanctity where we are and from our own state of life. Sanctity is not a matter of the privileged or consecrated, it is everyone's business.

Find holiness, work for it, offer work, thank for everything and from where we are, encourage those around us... This will give us the differential point to, little by little, bring about a positive change in our environment.

Remember that Jesus wants us to be saints in our vocation, it is a good way to be happy. God does not ask us the impossible, if not love, dedication and bearing fruit according to our state of life, although it may seem that we are no longer capable of anything. Because in God's eyes, every detail, every glance to the sky, every prayer, is an expression of the eternal love that He gives us.

St. Josemaría, we ask you to intercede for us so we can be faithful and holy in our ordinary life, and faithful to our vocation.

Jesus, I trust in You.

53. Saint Thérèse de Lisieux, the holiness that loves and offers itself to others

The well-known French saint gave us an extraordinary testimony of offering, desire to be with Jesus, of innocence, of love. Observing her, we realize how long is still left for us to go, and how much we can improve in our Christian life.

It's not a matter of age, it's a matter of love. Do we love God truly? Or, just when it is convenient to us? Do we trust Him?

Saint Thérèse lived faithfully her love towards the others, offering the small pains of life for those who needed it the most, for sinners, for the priests. And, moreover, with the desire not to stop and also to do good from eternity. Incredible wishes for an incredible family.

Learning from Saint Thérèse is learning from a disciple who always showed simplicity and humility; her love was so strong that she did not want to wait, she always wanted to offer herself without reservation.

We ask her and the saints for their intervention, to help us to be faithful and eager in love.

Saint Thérèse de Lisieux, please intercede for us so we know how to offer our everyday crosses for those who need it most.

Jesus, I trust in You.

54. Saint Anthony Mary Claret and Saint Paul, the holiness of bringing the Gospel to the world

The urgency of explaining the Gospel and bringing it to the world is explained by the brevity of life. St Anthony Mary Claret at one time and Saint Paul in another are two clear examples that, whether one has been lucky enough to be a Christian since childhood, or not, when Jesus is thoroughly acquainted, there is a great fire inside us, that people with communicative charisma need to announce the good news around the world.

Today many people develop this task in social networks, because it is where people are. And each period needs a voice to remember the unconditional love of God towards us.

It impacts us that saints of all times, touched by the untiring love of God, keep on preaching until exhaustion and endangering their lives, the commandment of love and the Gospel. Let us pray that new and holy vocations come out and we feel that it is everyone's responsibility to bring the Gospel to a world that every generation needs.

St Anthony Mary and St Paul, intercede for us so we know how to be bearers of the Gospel.

Jesus, I trust in You.

55. Saint John of God and Mother Teresa, the holiness of loving the forgotten

They got to the point of calling Saint John of God the madman of Granada, many did not understand his love for God directed towards the abandoned. This is what Mother Teresa said, the option for the poorest of the poor.

We realize that great saints have had the main source of strength in Holy Mass, so they could then carry out a titanic action of love towards the disabled and the forgotten, without which the world would feel at a loss.

Many hospitals today are named after Saint John of God. The reason is simple: when a person has an unlimited love, without schedule, this love transfers generations, because it comes from God.

We ask Saint John of God and Mother Teresa to make us sensitive to the neglected people we find along the way, to make us know how to be courageous enough to love and that we always know how to find strength in Jesus revived through Mass.

St John of God and Mother Teresa of Calcutta, intercede for us so we know how to love the neglected.

Jesus, I trust in You.

56. Saint Faustina Kowalska and Saint John Paul II, the holiness of bringing the mercy of God to the world

St Faustina was chosen by God, together with Saint John Paul II, to bring and promote the message of mercy to humanity. Two Polish saints. The first, received from Jesus the message of mercy. The second one, was in charge of culminating and bringing the captivating message of mercy to the world.

Our God is a close God who loves us, who wants the best for us, who wants to lead us towards love and reconcile this relationship every time we move away.

That is why mercy is so important in the recent history of the Church. Without it the multitude of meetings with Jesus, our prayer for the enemies, the compassion that makes Jesus say "forgive them, Father, they do not know what they are doing" can't be properly understood.

The mercy of God is manifested through trust. Confidence to know that God has the last word, the story has a good ending and we just have to say yes and act accordingly.

Mercy is important today and we have already emphasized the prayer of the Chaplet of the Divine Mercy, the "Jesus, I trust in You" and the image of the risen and merciful Jesus that spills His love unceasingly towards us.

That is why He especially invites us to the Eucharist, where we can find Him more easily and where we can receive communion because we cover ourselves with the merciful love of God.

St Faustina and St John Paul II, please pray for us to be compassionate and benign with our neighbours, and humble and courageous to ask God for forgiveness, whenever necessary.

Jesus, I trust in You.

57. Saint Pius X, the sanctity of promoting the Eucharist

We have widely talked in this book about the most important devotion: the Holy Mass. And Saint Pius X, the Pope, Joseph Sartre, took note of the importance of the Eucharist in the Christian life and the centrality of it as the motto "Establish everything in Christ". There is no other way without the Eucharist.

And to understand the value, fullness and depth of the Eucharistic sacrament, it is especially necessary catechesis, formation, correct communication of the mystery, to understand now and at all times that Jesus is present in Holy Mass and that we are privileged to share the table with the resurrected Savior.

St. Pius X, of humble origin, did not get tired of looking for the way to approach the believers to Holy Mass and to clearly explain the strength of it. A Mass that is a source of peace and unity.

Promoting the Eucharist and the education in the faith is, briefly, bearing and living the good news through word and work, an act of supreme charity and source of all charity acts.

St. Pius X, intercede for us, so that we may always be devotees of the Eucharist and show the love of God to others, through word and through work.

Jesus, I trust in You.

58. Saint Joseph, holiness in fidelity

In St. Joseph we find loyalty, patience, love, knowing how to listen to God with simplicity. We find the ideal virtues of a holiness that does not seek recognition, but to make Christ be recognized, and to feel dignified by it.

St Joseph is a great model, a model of how a good person should be, patient, more concerned about the purpose of life than the legitimate personal interests that he could have. The mission was so great that he carried it out with conviction and determination, helping the Virgin Mary and Jesus. He lived the role he was going to play without making any noise.

It is the role of many Christians to be persevering in the small acts of love, without stridences but, after all, necessary acts, so that the world can carry forward in the progress of knowing how to love.

Saint Joseph listened to God because he was in full disposition. So we have to be ourselves, always ready to love as much as necessary. Even when we feel despised.

St. Joseph, intercede for us, so we know how to be faithful to God in our daily lives.

Jesus, I trust in You.

59 Saint Augustine, the sanctity of rectification

St. Augustine sought the truth but walked in the error. For many years it was like this. But his mother, St Monica, did not get tired of praying for her son. Before conversion, he had lived irregularly in the company of a woman, had a son and joined an heretical sect.

St Monica's key role, is that she never stopped praying for her son. A key role, too, for us, is not to get tired of praying for our relatives and, especially, for those who need it most.

St. Augustine converted reading St. Paul's letters, listening to St. Ambròs, reading the conversion story of a great pagan speaker... but, above all, thanks to the tireless prayer of his mother.

After his conversion, one of the great hardships that Augustine had to overcome was living in chastity, despite wanting to follow God without reservations. One day, while praying to God to help him with purity, he heard the voice of a singing child: take and read, take and read... Augustine, inspired by these words, opened the Sacred Scripture at random and found a fragment of the letter of the Epistle to the Romans (Romans 13, 13-14), which says:

13 So behave properly, as people do in the day. Don't go to wild parties or get drunk or be vulgar or indecent. Don't quarrel or be jealous. 14 Let the Lord Jesus Christ be as near to you as the clothes you wear. Then you won't try to satisfy your selfish desires.

This event definitively marked Saint Augustine's life and was able to keep his chastity for the rest of his life, becoming Bishop of Hippo and helping many find and live the Gospel.

Let us consider that reaching the top of any virtue comes after a humble and sincere prayer to God. And then, once you live the virtues, you can do good with the word and the work. With that same word Saint Augustine wrote numerous books such as Confessions or The City of God.

There's one famous sentence from St. Augustine: "You have made us for Yourself, oh Lord, and our heart is restless until it rests in You". And the saint of Hippo took a long time to live this rest until he finally found it. It is never too late to find the rest of God and live in His grace.

St Augustine and St Monica, we pray for you to intercede for us, so we know how to always seek the truth with sincerity and do not get tired of praying for our relatives and friends who need it most, so that we can all experience the virtues with joy.

Jesus, I trust in You.

60. Saint Joaquina Vedruna de Mas, the sanctity of educating, caring and loving others

Santa Joaquina did not just educate her own children. Her vocation for love, charity and education led to the fact that, once widowed, she became a nun and founded the Carmelites of Charity, dedicated to education and assistance to the ill.

In society, the weakest are those who have no education, and the sick. St Joaquina anwered with generosity to God's calling, despite her preferences for a contemplative life. She was always humble to the dispositions of the spiritual directors and she did not save energies for herself, only for the heroic lifestyle of charity.

St Joaquina is an example of that strong mother who not only dedicates herself in body and soul to the family, but her love is so great too that it even goes beyond family.

St Joaquina was a pioneer in educational and assistance needs. An example for us, a reflection of the humbleness of Mary to fulfill the will of God at all times.

St Joaquina Vedruna, please intercede for us, so we know how to be generous and sensitive to educate the uneducated and properly attend those who need it.

Jesus, I trust in You.

Final words (the Epistle of Paul to the Colossians 3, 12-17)

12 God loves you and has chosen you as his own special people. So be gentle, kind, humble, meek, and patient.
13 Put up with each other, and forgive anyone who does you wrong, just as Christ has forgiven you.
14 Love is more important than anything else. It is what ties everything completely together.
15 Each one of you is part of the body of Christ, and you were chosen to live together in peace. So let the peace that comes from Christ control your thoughts. And be grateful. 16 Let the message about Christ completely fill your lives, while you use all your wisdom to teach and instruct each other. With thankful hearts, sing psalms, hymns, and spiritual songs to God.
17 Whatever you say or do should be done in the name of the Lord Jesus, as you give thanks to God the Father because of him.

Final prayer

Glory to God in the highest,
and peace to His people on earth.
Lord God, heavenly King,
Almighty God and Father,
we worship You, we give You thanks,
we praise You for Your glory.
Lord Jesus Christ,
only Son of the Father,
Lord God, Lamb of God,
You take away the sin of the world:
have mercy on us;
You are seated at the right hand of the Father:
receive our prayer.
For You alone are the Holy One,
You alone are the Lord,
You alone are the Most High,
Jesus Christ, with the Holy Spirit,
in the glory of the Father.

Amen.

Annex: Look at Jesus face to face

Adoring the Blessed Sacrament is to be with Jesus, with Jesus face to face, present in the sacred bread. The real presence of Jesus in the Eucharist stays with us in Adoration to the Most Holy.

When we adore Jesus, we sometimes talk about worshipping the Eucharist or worshipping the Blessed Sacrament. There are different ways of saying the same.

Jesus is alive. Adoration to the Most Holy gives us a stronger, deeper view of God, of our God who lives and wants to be always with us. In worship, we can praise God, give thanks, meditate, contemplate, ask for forgiveness, heal, share our needs... We are with Jesus, true God and true man, and we have a relationship of loving friendship with Him.

If our spiritual life does not progress, we find in Adoration to Jesus a new advance.

That is why I consider it essential that we promote and make known the Eucharistic Adoration and, above all, that we do Adoration as far as we can. We will receive grace after grace. It is the love of Jesus towards us.

I have been in chapels of Eucharistic Adoration. There I have noticed the real presence of God within me, His company, His strength, His love and His mercy. A desire to love Him better, and to love others better too. A boost of faith.

Therefore, one of the great moments to awaken our faith, perhaps one of the greatest, is to be with Christ the Eucharist face to face and to be able to worship Him. He will give us love so that we can then be loving each other with authentic charity and heartfelt sincerity.

Without a doubt, adoring the Most Holy may be the most decisive push in our faith and the spiritual progress of a Catholic, because Jesus, with His mercy, wants us to heal our deepest and most hidden wounds.

Our life in faith is like a watch. The clock of faith. In this metaphor, if we put the Jesus in the center, imagine above, at 12, the Holy Mass; below, at 6, Adoration to the Most Holy. On the right, at 3, the mercy we receive in the sacrament of forgiveness. And to the left, at 9, the charity that we can give thanks to the mercy received and the impulse of the Eucharist by the delivery of our talents and our love. If our heart revolves around this watch, our time will be loving and will bear abundant fruits. And we will walk towards the dynamic "mercy, Eucharist, mercy"...

Where do you worship Jesus?

More and more parishes, chapels or churches exhibit the Blessed Sacrament, sometimes with holy hours, sometimes before or after Mass, sometimes once a week, or even all day long in chapels of Perpetual Adoration.

Also on the internet, in case you can not physically attend, several channels of YouTube, such as Catholify (from Birmingham, Alabama, USA), show Jesus on the Blessed Sacrament permanently, 24 hours a day.

"If you want to find God, look at Jesus in the Blessed Sacrament"

This is the advice that Sair del Toro received. Sair lived a Catholic childhood, but in adolescence, like so many, she abandoned faith. She then had a successful life, with her own radio show and as a wedding planner in Seattle (United States).

But fame and money did not give her what she needed, to feel love in the deepest extent. She felt empty. For this reason, she decided to return to God's side and to the Church. They advised her to look at the Blessed Sacrament, that is, to find herself directly with the resurrected and healing Jesus.

She followed the advice, entered an adoration chapel and felt something extraordinary:

"I entered, I embraced Jesus Christ, and He came out and embraced me. I felt his presence in my heart, in my mind and in my soul, He was embracing me. It was the biggest hug in all my life".

She explains that this moment completely changed her life. She left her job, her previous life and went to a convent of nuns in Omaha. So much so that her mother, who had educated her Catholic, seeing the change so suddenly, sent her to the psychiatrist. The doctor determined that she had no problems, she simply fell in love with God.

After a discernment, she left the United States and returned to her native Mexico. There she worked in the evangelization and devotion to the Sacred Heart of Jesus. In 2013 she returned to the United States to teach couples the Theology of the Body of Saint John Paul II in the diocese of Los Angeles. She combines this minister with an evangelization of people who do not walk centered in life: prisoners, violent people… achieving that many of them consecrate their life and their family to God and marking a radical change with their previous lifestyle. She also works at the Magnífica Foundation (https://magnifica.com.mx/), in support of women.

An example of the miracles that have happened in her task of help is the case of Rachel (fictitious name) that was kidnapped and sold from Mexico to the United States. The kidnappers abused her and she had two children while living in captivity, until a neighbor alerted the police and they were able to rescue her. Now she's trying to heal inside Magnífica with Sair's help and work.

And to think that all these miracles and profound changes began by looking and embracing Jesus in the Blessed Sacrament...

Sair says: "My goal is Heaven and I want to be holy, I really want to be holy. So I relax, letting God do what He wants with me."

So, we can abandon ourselves to God's will, so it can be fulfilled. And we can say to Jesus, as Saint Teresa of Jesus said: "I am Yours and born for You, what do You want of me?".

Made in the USA
Middletown, DE
20 August 2022

71822714R00099